Ethics Of The Homestead Strike

Ethics of the Homestead Strike : A Narrative by the Wayside.

A reporter attached to one of the great Western journals sought one day to enter the village of Homestead. The town in the hands of the strikers offered a rare opportunity for the exercise of his peculiar genius. He was not an ordinary reporter on the scent for a sensation or earliest news. He was bidden : "Go and without haste thoroughly canvass the situation. Make a study of the whole problem, if you can. Get at facts. Seek interviews with the managers of the steel works, and with the coolest, most intelligent of the strikers. Gather all the ins and outs and form a judgment. Send that to us whenever you are yourself satisfied with it." This, in substance, was his commission. The journal he represented had for its editor a gentleman of rare intelligence. Moreover, he had come to the disposition to consider the labor problem seriously. He had arrived at this state of mind slowly. For a long time he had stoutly maintained that there was no such thing as a labor problem in any new sense of the term. Always there had been a problem easy of solution. Labor and capital alike were under the law of supply and demand. The problem settled itself. It was a question of arithmetic. The ethical element consisted simply of fair play in competition. After that, " Devil take the hindmost." The annual outbreaks—the differences employers and employees fell into—had no significance outside of this : With which party is the most staying power ? Right reducible to the question of might.

There was nothing singular in this position. All the world, apparently, accepted it—the striker no less than the capitalist. He had inherited this opinion with a thousand others which he had seen no reason to change. It was common sense from the purely intellectual standpoint. Though his feelings had sometimes rebelled, it was easy to persuade himself that they were in a rebellion that should be put down.

He had been editor ten years.

Going home one night with the news of the Homestead strike, his wife asked : " How do you think it will turn out ?"

" The Amalgamated Union is strong, but Carnegie will beat it."

" I shall be sorry if that prophecy comes true," replied the wife, thoughtfully.

" Why sorry ? Don't you desire things to take their natural course ? Sorry ? Yes, in a sense. As one is sorry when an earthquake upsets a town and swallows people. Sorry for the individuals concerned. But thankful, my dear, that the whole country is not burst asunder and the whole population doomed. The order of nature must go on, and does go on for the general good, despite the occasional sacrifice of individuals.

3

Same law governs the strike. If Carnegie wins, the union fellows go out and non-union men go in. Why more sorry for union than non-union? They are all human beings, equally naked and equally hungry. It's absurd to take sides. You yourself often say, 'Why take sides in a ball game or race of any kind? Let the best side win. I have no other favorites.' So say I."

"I hardly think you do so say in the case of the strike. It isn't which is *best*, but which is the most needy—union or non-union men. In other words, Carnegie stands by smiling—no danger of his starving for a thousand years yet. He says: 'You Amalgamated Union men have resources. You can live without wages a year or so. But there are plenty whose necessities will drive them into our mills on our terms.'"

"Yes, and these Amalgamated men retort: 'We will beat back or kill every man who dares show himself on these grounds.' When the strike reaches that point, government interferes, puts the strikers in jail, and so the matter ends."

The wife made no reply at the time. But, as she said good-night when the editor went forth to his duties, she gently added these words: "If you really think, 'So the matter ends,' your thinking ends a very long ways from the end, I assure you."

The editor smiled a little half smile and hurried on to his task. The parting shot his wife had given him had, seemingly, missed its mark. Preoccupied with a matter of immediate personal interest, he lost sight of whatever other consideration. For some days he had revolved in his mind a little labor problem of his own.

He had wished to wind up his ten years of editorial service with the acquisition of a greater editorial freedom. The *Western Commonwealth* needed, in his judgment, a new impetus. He alone should be charged with the responsibility. He wished the editorial department to cover a wider range of topics, to be treated with all the seriousness and interested ability he could command. He would return to the old Greeley way and edit his paper under the inspiration of convictions: make the *Commonwealth*, like the elder *Tribune*, the repository of ideas.

He had communicated his plan to the board of directors. And this night on which he had been told by the intuitive mind of the woman he loved that he had not thought to the end of a problem he had so long dismissed as being no problem at all, he was informed by the directors whose opinion he had affected to despise that if he wished to bring the journal whose interests he had so much at heart to the forefront of American journalism, he "must launch at once, and that without fear or favor, the great and henceforth all-absorbing question of labor and capital."

The note lay before him on his desk.

He had carefully reread it.

It gave him full discretion: "We give you one year for the trial. Do not take sides. Enter on the discussion as upon any other question of science. Treat the capitalist as you do the

4

laborer, the laborer as the capitalist; both without reserve. The interests of neither class are in the problem. It is a question of common weal to be settled on a basis of equity."

"*To be settled on a basis of equity.*" He sat there repeating the words. These commonplace, worldly-minded directors! What had come over the spirit of their dreams? "Perhaps they think they scent a coming revolution, a Socialistic propaganda, and have hit on the idea that there's money in it. They want to make the great *Western Commonwealth* over into an organ of the People's Party, perchance. The People's Party, forsooth! And give me *carte blanche* to try the experiment one year. I think I'll fool them. I *will* discuss the 'labor question.' I'll ride it to death. I'll show it up as it never was shown up before. I'll plant myself on facts indisputable and logic impregnable. For one year! I accept my freedom."

The editor went home early that night.

"My advice is," quoth the wife, "that you take a month to think the matter over before you open your mouth or commit yourself."

There was no harm in that. He was in no hurry. A few editorials such as he intended to write would do the business—and he had a whole year!

It was strange.

The next day he could think of nothing else; nor the day after; nor for many days after that. It was labor—labor reform—capital and labor—the "all-absorbing topic."

Even his dreams were disturbed. The very nightmare of labor problems was upon him and brooded o'er him. He woke his wife crying: "The Pinkertons—the Pinkertons are coming!" He saw vast armies, and saw himself in the front ranks, breasting the shocks of battle.

He could not wait his month out.

He must set about his task, and at once.

Here again a suggestion from his good wife led the way and directed his course: "Send Swinton to Homestead."

Silas Parringham at last agreed with his wife. There *was* a labor problem unsolved.

And young Swinton was his right-hand man—his reporter in the field.

He gave Swinton his commission and sent him forth.

A week and no report.

Parringham was uneasy, but his wife counseled patience.

Patience won the day.

Swinton could take all the time he pleased.

In taking time Swinton was but following instructions. He intended to take the matter leisurely, for he was commanded not only to gather facts, but to elaborate his own idea of the situation. He asked himself: "What, anyhow, is at the bottom of all this labor business?" And he proposed to answer that question, using the Homestead disturbance, so far as he found it available, as illustration.

It was three weeks before he sent to the editor of the *Western Commonwealth* his study of the labor problem from the Homestead point of view.

When Editor Parringham opened the document—its bulk fully justifying the term—his wife was standing by. Her eye first caught the significance of the title : "*Ethics* of the Homestead Strike."

"That sounds something like it !" she exclaimed. "I shall be interested. You may depend upon it Swinton is a true radical—he probes to the root of the matter. There is *nothing* in human affairs but has an ethical basis."

"We will take the document home," said Editor Parringham, "where we can go through it without interruption."

Late that night they were still absorbed in its contents. The small hours of the morning struck before they had finished. The reading of the document itself consumed but part of the time. There had been long intervals of earnest, not to say exciting, discussion—Editor Parringham questioning with great emphasis most of Swinton's "advanced ideas," saying, "He's gone mad. Talks like a lunatic. He's no better than an anarchist." The wife gently defends the young reporter, and avows that she sees in his document "the first gleams of equity, like a sun rising out of the mist."

"Pshaw !" the editor responds, and the reading is continued.

It appeared that Swinton, on the day he made his appearance in Homestead, had been taken into custody by the police of the strikers. He had no little difficulty in convincing those sturdy knights of labor that he was not a Pinkerton in disguise. It was not until one of the leaders appeared on the scene that he got his statement accepted. Then he was furnished with a little " permit " to go and come as he pleased. He went into the mills, but Frick and his managers had little to communicate. He talked with leading strikers, but gained nothing more than was already well known. One sentence only fell from the lips of one man which lingered in his mind : " Our strike has a future significance far greater than the present need, considered alone, justifies. Were we calculating interests merely from the standpoint of the present, the reduction proposed might have been accepted with a protest. But we were convinced that this was but the opening for further reductions that would result disastrously to us. Hence, after full and solemn consideration of the case, we decided to make our fight at the outset, while we were strong and the probabilities of success were as nine to one."

"So," said Swinton, responding to this statement, " after all said to the contrary, there *is* antagonism between capital and labor. Two hostile camps, both organized, disciplined, and ever watchful."

"You can depend on that from the word go. Capital is *always* greedy. That is its nature."

"And labor ?"

"Wants all it can get. Why not ? The lesson of this life is to look out for number one."

For a number of days Swinton went his way among the people of the town, questioning some, but listening more. And from all sides came the assurance that the relation of capital and labor was naturally, inevitably, a state of war.

6

"There's no love lost between us, you can bet, and never was. The managers look out for their interests, and we for ours. If they see an opening, they don't pass it by with eyes averted. Neither do we. It's very nice for Carnegie to keep us down to living wages, and then toss us a library. He gets a great name for his charities—philanthropies. But if we need his gifts, we ought to be able to earn them for ourselves. That fact alone shows that at best we are underpaid. How is it that capital has all it wants and to spare, while labor must ever go begging? They say it's 'brains.' Heaven preserve us! Look at the skilled men toiling there in the mills! Brains, forsooth! Carnegie might toss his into balance and be found wanting."

It was a woman who spoke.

Indeed, Swinton began to think that he must consult women only if he was ever to get down to any practical discussion of the real issue. But one day he met a man somewhat advanced in years who seemed quite disposed to unburden himself. He was of the strikers, but only through sympathy. Not a steel-worker, but a day-laborer, in fact. So he confessed. Swinton was struck by his appearance, and their little conversation as they walked a block or two caused him to be more anxious than he had hitherto been in waiting upon the so-called leaders to secure an extended interview.

"Let us go down to the river-bank, where we can talk in quiet," said his companion, seeming to divine his own heart's wish. "We hain't got to the true inwardness of this thing yet," he continued. "I have my ideas, but if I was to give 'em out Homestead would quickly be made too hot for me to stay in—if, indeed, I got out with a whole skin. So, if I unburden to you, you must keep *me* out of it. Swear to that."

"I swear!" cried Swinton, keeping his half smile to himself.

"Then grace and mercy defend you!" said the man solemnly ; a moment later adding, "as the Scriptures say."

Swinton was not up in sacred literature, but somehow it seemed to him that he could locate the quotation elsewhere. However, without comment, he suffered himself to be led to the river's bank.

The river flowed by peacefully. The sunlight lay on its surface a gold-and-silver sheen. They stood a moment silently regarding its beauty.

"Many a time," said the man, as he threw himself on the grassy bank—"many a time I've been down here alone by myself to think over this business of labor. Nature somehow lets a man think. I have come to the conclusion that our fellows are going wrong in some of their methods ; but what else can they do to keep from going to the wall? I don't just see. Where would they have been but for their organization? Don't you suppose they have forced up their wage and kept it up? No fight between capital and labor, you say? What's all the fuss about, then? Why are the men out on a strike? Yes, there *can* be peace. Take what's set before you and hold your tongue. There could be a mighty peaceful time here in Homestead if the workers would only let Frick have it all his own way. But the lamb would soon be in the lion's belly. That's one way to end the war—end open hostilities, I mean. Workingmen would simply stay conquered. But 'tain't in the nature of man here in America, anyhow, to so quiet down into submission and slavery. If you don't help yourself, God help you! But no, he never does. Just the contrary. He helps them as helps themselves. At least, so the preachers say. Now, I've been thinking—what is the matter? There *is* antagonism between laborers and capitalists; but why *should* there be? We ain't working it right, somehow. You talk about a fair day's pay for a fair day's work. But what *is* fair? Who knows? Who can tell? Ask Carnegie? Ask O'Donnell? What will Carnegie answer? He'll say, 'Whatever I can afford to pay.' What will O'Donnell answer? 'Enough to keep me and mine properly clothed, fed and schooled.' They mayn't put it just that way, but that's about the substance of both answers. But you see you get nowhere. You're no nearer knowing what's *fair* than you was before. What's Carnegie's 'afford to pay' mean? It don't settle the honesty, the equity, of the thing. If he can't afford to pay—well, what's the use of talking? When a man can't afford to do the right thing, he can go out of business. But to say the *right* can be measured by what one can *afford* is absurd. And O'Donnell is just as far from the point. He wants a wage equal to his *needs*. But there again you're all at sea. A man's needs! A *fair* wage will cover them, will it? Of course, every man ought to be able to make a good living. But he must balance his living, his needs, by the service he renders. In demanding his wage, he ought to be able to say what is *honestly* due him, and regulate his *needs* accordingly. So it comes to this in my mind: what can a man take for the labor he does and not do other men injustice? In other words, we come round again to the old question, What *is* a fair day's work and a fair day's pay? Neither Carnegie nor O'Donnell have offered satisfactory answers."

"But the strikers are safe in saying they are not overpaid, at least—on general principles, that is?"

Swinton interposed this question, not quite getting the drift of the old man's talk, and feeling that he was a trifle prosy.

"To keep to the practical side of the matter," he added, "if we agree that the strikers are not making an unreasonable demand, what is your objection to their method of enforcing it? You say it is war. There are no laws in war. Do what will *win* is the only rule."

The old man looked puzzled a moment, and then answered:

"Well, I see we shall have to call for a division of the question, as they say in Congress. The Homestead strike is one thing, and the labor question is another thing. The one deals with a present emergency; the other stretches along into the future and deals with principles. Let us take up the strike first.

"Now, mind you, I don't oppose the strike. As matters stood, men could not stop to build up an ideal standard of what was fair. They must take it for granted that they were not getting any too much of a return for their labor, and smite the enemy hip and thigh. They were forced into a fight, and they must make the best of it.

"I regret that workingmen do not all pull together. If there were no non-union men, the workers would simply control the matter of wage to suit themselves. But that cannot be expected, since the union practically is limited in numbers to the demand for workers. It can't offer the same inducements as Carnegie. If it undertook the support of all unable to get employment, it would soon have an army of idlers on its hands. It is useless to appeal to the unemployed and say : 'Please remain unemployed and leave the job to us.' Every such man must say in reply : 'It's sink or swim with me. If you swim out, I swim in.' He may not like Carnegie any better than union men do, but he must take the chance to save self from idleness and starvation when it comes in sight. He cannot be expected to be less selfish than his brother of the union is. So the success of a strike lies in there not being enough outside men to fill the strikers' places. They hold the key to the situation so long as they keep this surplus down. By refusing to work with non-union men, the mills cannot run unless there are non-union men in sufficient numbers to run them. Manager Frick knows this pinch but too well, and has waged unrelenting war on the Amalgamated Union from the start. He hates it, of course. If he can break it up, and deal with the men as individuals, he will have everything practically in his own hands.

"Naturally, one says, that should be the way. Man with man. Every man competent to make his own bargain. But it all depends. The world has learned but too well the lesson of strength only in union. Napoleon won his battles by fighting his enemy piecemeal, so to speak. That's what Frick wants to do—confessing thus that the workingmen *are* an enemy. If he can get at them singly or in squads, all's well. He has them in his power. The union grows up naturally enough, then—not to abridge any man's making his own contract, but to make a contract possible. The parties to a contract must be equals, or as nearly so as possible. When one is weak and the other strong, it is simply dictation. Frick says he will not suffer dictation. No more should the workingman. But his only chance to make himself the manager's equal is to shake hands with his brother workman, and with him make some sort of treaty of defence, or offence. if the case demands. It were a long story to go into this matter of dealing alone with individuals. It sounds well, and strikes the American ear pleasantly. It gives Manager Frick a certain prestige with the public. All your small editors re-echo it as though 'twere law and gospel both. But let one of those editors put himself in the place of a poor workman applying singly, going as an individual alone to make his bargain with Manager Frick, and he'd soon find out the pitiable condition his individualism had brought him to. He, one individual, standing there without a cent in his pocket ; another individual just out the door, in desperate straits, waiting for him to come out that he may himself go in and accept the

9

humiliation he had refused. Manager Frick sitting there cool, serene—with his own and Carnegie's millions behind him. Is that a picture of equality between individuals? No. To be Frick's equal in making the contract, the workman must have a backing equal to Frick's. It's a state of war, and you mustn't forget it. The union is trying to offset in some proportion the superior strength of capital's manager. It is true that the union is despotic. The individual has surrendered to it the right of making contract. He owes it allegiance, pays his taxes, and submits. What else do you do in submitting to your republican government, with its coercion laws, protective tariffs, and thousand other laws as despotic in their nature as any czar of Russia can fulminate? The *unions* are all alike. What was your war under Lincoln but a war against *non*-union men? The Amalgamated within its own sphere is only a plagiarist of your Federal Union. Does the State government of Pennsylvania allow a non-union man to exist outside of a jail? And yet it turns around and says to the Homestead strikers : 'The right of private, individual contract is sacred. You must interfere with no man's freedom.' To be consistent, it should establish and defend a 'union' for every trade or branch of business. Yet, forsooth, it sends its General Snowden here, to put down every attempt of workingmen to fashion their protective unions after the pattern the State itself has set. It comes to protect life and property? But when did the State have regard for either if its own needs imaginary or otherwise required the taking of either? Life, liberty, property, are all at the mercy of the State union. How was it? Did this army of Snowden's come here under private contract? If the men enlisted freely, did they not agree to obey the commanding general? And if one of them does not, what is his reward? He may be shot or—hung up by the ears.

"I am not here and now quarreling with this state of things. I say only that the 'despotism' of the union grows out of the situation just as naturally as does that of the State. And its aim is quite as high. It is organized not to defraud or injure individual members, but to protect and secure them the advantages of freedom from the oppressions of the common enemy. Its officers may make mistakes, or sometimes o'erstep their delegated authority. Are your statesmen, politicians, your State officials, free from all suspicion in that respect?

"I, then, under the circumstances, stand for the union, and am not a friend of the non-union men seeking to help Carnegie out of his scrape.

"But, at the same time, I think it bad policy to enter on a contest with the State authorities. If the despotic State says the non-union men must be permitted to go and come freely from the mills, why, so be it. We must acquiesce. We have got to in the end, and we may as well do so at the beginning. As to the fight with the Pinkertons, I'm not, on the whole, sorry it occurred. It has brought that whole business before the country with too much emphasis to permit of its ever being laid aside unsettled. The Pinkertons must go.

"But, as a matter of fact, the Pinkertons summoned by Frick

came here to do precisely what the militia are doing—stop strikers from interfering to prevent new men from entering the mills. Why, then, should the strikers welcome Snowden? They got the rebuff they deserved. Why pretend to be law-abiding men, as the phrase goes, when they were not and had no intention of being? No non-union man was to be allowed to enter the mills. The strikers took possession of the town and intended to hold it until Frick was subdued. It was a foolish thing to do. Frick had the law on his side, and sooner or later, if he could not get the Pinkertons, he could summon the Governor and his militia; and if that was not enough, the Governor could call on the President, and he could summon the whole country. Public opinion was against us on that score. We were defeated from the start. We had finally to yield ignominiously. We had done better never to have placed ourselves in the situation. We should have confined ourselves to personal appeal, or been sure that our places could not be filled. That was, that is, our only chance. If we succeed finally, it will be because non-union men cannot or will not step into our shoes. So much for the strike. Now, as to the labor question, it is high time public attention was turned seriously toward a better understanding of it."

Swinton had given himself up to be a listener. "Let the old man talk," he said to himself; "I'll give an attent ear, and make the most of it." But it was hardly possible simply to listen. His own mind was in motion, following out threads of discussion for which his companion was at least furnishing suggestive if not startling texts. One conclusion he had arrived at already, and, interrupting the other's monologue, he made this avowal: "If you will permit me—I am fully persuaded that the strike, successful or otherwise, settles nothing. The real issue is not even touched. Whichever side is defeated, it will surrender not to a principle or natural law discovered that puts the dispute on an ethical basis, and so disposes of it forever."

"Precisely so," the old man interrupted, speaking with emphasis. "That was my reason for dividing the subject. And my complaint of workingmen generally is that they will waste all their time and energy in these, comparatively speaking, barren struggles with capitalists. If the Amalgamated Steel Workers would devote one-tenth of their means to the effort at placing their cause on its moral legs, if I may so speak, I should have far more respect for and faith in them. But they don't seem to see that—only in a general way. 'We don't get pay enough,' they growl; but what *is* enough? They don't know or seem to care. Like Frick, they will take all they can get, all they can stagger under. It may be a hard thing to say, but, as a matter of fact, I don't know one of them who would not step into Frick's shoes if he could, and do about the same as he has done. So it remains with them a matter only of ins and outs."

"Well, we are agreed on that. Now, what is your solution?"

"Mine? I can't say as I have any as yet; but I have been thinking. To plump it right out as I keep feeling it, and sometimes seeing it, I say it is *the giving up the idea of the power of capital to increase on itself*. Whatever shape it takes—profit, interest, rent—I use the terms in the every-day meaning of them—capital is turned into a monster that eats up all before it. The hardest thing, we are told, is to get your *first one thousand dollars*. After that, increase comes easier. Why? Because your capital works for you; gives an advantage over your fellow-workers. It goes out and returns laden with the fruits of their labor. Get a few thousand and you may begin your career of sitting in your office with a clerk to gather in the spoils.

"An *office* is a great thing. A *man* in an office is a greater wonder. He is no longer the simple individual you have known, neighborly and considerate. He is on his nerve. You call, and he looks up with his ' Well, sir, what can I do for you?' He is busy figuring his income. He has rents here, and loans there, and no end of investments. He works hard. No doubt of that. And every laborer is worthy of his hire—or if he isn't, he ought to be. Depends on how you take it. The highwayman lives a hard life; no one works harder than your professional burglar.

"Suppose we follow up the career of this man in the office and see what comes of it.

"He is an agent at first; a broker; a go-between; does business for other people and gets his commission. Trains for himself a sharp eye for good chances. Knows how to invest, and where. After a little, he invests for himself. Puts money into a lot. Waits for others to do the same in his neighborhood. Ten years, and he will sell it. Double, thribble—no telling where the increase will stop. Other like investments follow. He builds houses; rent flows in. The house is paid for in rent. Ten years has done it over and above all cost of repairing. In ten years that house duplicates itself. Ten years more, four houses. Ten more years, eight houses—all paying rent. All this over and above wear and tear. He has eat his cake and kept it; much better. I have said nothing of the increased valuation of his property. And what has it all cost him? Little or no personal attention. Only the hire of a clerk. Or, suppose it occupied his whole time, and he labored each day as many hours as any man ought to. The difference between his labor and other men's labor who have no capital working for them is not so great. But they remain poor. He grows rich. His investments have done it. Capital has made him the rich man that he is; not his labor, not his brains. Other men's brains are as good as his, and they have worked as hard.

"If this man in the office goes into business, it is the same thing. Capital does it. How does he figure? So much per cent profit for capital—over all cost, his own salary included. That is, he pays himself for his labor, and then deducts from the sum due others for their labor enough to make up the per cent he claims for the use of his capital. That is the way he amasses wealth, grows rich. It is the capital that works for him that does it."

"Well, so far as I at present see," Swinton interrupts, "that seems all right. And yet—"

"*And yet!*" exclaims the old man. "That 'and yet' tells the story of the future. Your instincts tell you that what seems all right may not be all right, after all. Let us go on.

"Now, what is there to be said against this increase of capital? Inevitably it builds up large fortunes for the few and leaves the many living from hand ,to mouth. The producers—the workingmen—pay tribute. The manipulators—the barons—build of this tribute fine castles, wear fine linen and live sumptuously every day. I'm not sure but things average up, so far as happiness goes, and the children of the poor turn out possibly as well as those of the rich. But it would be better to avoid either extreme. Making all allowance for difference of ability, the greater or less capacity shown, it does not seem that naturally there would be so wide a divergence in the results of men's labor. Investigate the matter and you see it is, in fact, the outcome of this tariff which capital imposes on labor.

"This great inequality of fortunes, on the face of it, is, to say the least, not democratic. Yearly there is growing up in this country an aristocracy of wealth. If the tendency is inevitable—if it is the sole and true outcome of the industrial problem—then your boasted free republican institutions go for very little. Titles cut no great figure as yet, but social lines and exclusions are to be found all the same. Your heiress and working-girl are as far asunder as princess and peasant girl. Yet your 'religion of humanity' no less than the Christian religion knows no such distinction. Which is right—your religion or your industrial system?

"It is urged that your millionaire gives back sooner or later, in one form or another,all the excess of wealth he has acquired over others. Possibly. But the question is, was it well for him to acquire it? Did it come into his possession fairly? Was it a 'fair day's work for a fair day's pay' he gave? Waiving that a moment—in a democratic land where the people boast their self government, the laborers ought all to share in contributing whatever public pleasure or benefit. The burden of acquiring and giving should be common. People who have things done for them lose half their value. The doing itself is the test of character. It implies intellectual activity; exercise of head and heart; ready and willing hands. How much higher the ideal of a community where all were participants—all able to do each his or her share! No need of a Carnegie library! No Carnegie possible as an industrial product!

"The Socialists, or one set of them, propose to turn the whole industrial system over to the State, and in that way balance accounts so that a more uniform or even distribution of wealth shall be brought about. But to my mind that would be like jumping from the frying-pan into the fire.

"Nor do I see any rational basis for the dream of the Nationalists. I have read 'Looking Backward.' To all such schemes I have one standing objection. They mean the destruction of individual independence. No man initiates his own enterprise. Everybody is busy planning for everybody else. The only justification attempted, so far as I know, for these proposals to subordinate and control the individual is that he is intensely selfish and his private interests are constantly antagonizing the public or general interest. By a system of co-operation improvised for the new era, this selfish nature is to be held duly in check, if not wholly subverted. My opinion is that the individual needs not to be *squelched*, but *enlightened*. Not many men can be won over to the idea that to succeed in life they must act without regard to self, or by ignoring their own private interests. On the contrary, private interests need far more attention. Every man should know definitely what his private or personal interest is. That is what he was individualized for. He must learn his relation to men and things. People think they must be born again, become eminently self-sacrificing, before they can come into true or harmonious relations with their fellows. But I would preach instead a gospel of self-aggrandizement, on the high plane of individual dignity, power, intelligence—aggrandizement that demands all the virtues, and consistent with the equality and freedom of all men. If we cannot build on the basis of the individual, we are like a house without foundation. When I say individual, it does not mean some particular individual, this or that fortunate one—a few, a part only, as some persist in thinking—those who have strength to forge ahead or climb to the top and tyrannize over their fellows. Individualism includes all. Every man, woman or child you meet is its representative. And the supposition is, at least, that each will find his or her highest interests in harmony with the good of all. If this is not so, democracy is a failure. Our ideal of universal opportunity, liberty, happiness, is a delusion ; the Declaration of Independence, as it was once called, a ' glittering generality ' only.

" For one, I believe in it, and in the *whole of mankind*. And I believe there is a solution of the industrial problem consistent with this noblest ideal. And I distrust at once every custom, however hoary with age, that tends to build up one man, or a class of men, at the expense of others. I throw my protecting thought around the world, and do not miss any one individual aspiring to manhood I do not say to the individual who in his blind impotency is striving to secure benefits for himself at the expense or to the injury of others, 'You sha'n't,' but I say emphatically, ' *You can't.*' If there be sacrifice, it must be mutual and complementary. You can ask no more than you give.

" But to come *once more* to the point."

Swinton, it must be confessed, was himself indulging a secret wish of this sort ; and yet the old man's energy, earnestness, enthusiasm, carried him along contentedly enough, and made him not averse to giving his friend ample scope and time for the development of his thought. It was interesting to meet with a *real believer*, anyhow. The atmosphere of the great city was so continuously skeptical, so like a London fog. His only anxiety was lest the old man should, after all, peter out and arrive with all his thinking at nowhere in particular. It puzzled him yet to see what he could mean by capital's not being endowed with the right of increase. He could think on the subject up to a certain point, and then he beat the air. Would the old man do the same? He was alert and eager, now that they were nearing the "point."

"All right," said he; "it is the point we are after. It has all been very interesting to me, but minus the 'point' it all goes by the board. Like a ship without a rudder, we sail nowhere in particular."

"You are quite right," replied his friend; "but it is difficult to state the point, or rather to restore it, clear away the rubbish of error the centuries have piled over it. For it must have been a very early idea of social man, because so simple and obvious, that among equals there could only in equity be an exchange of equal service—burden borne for burden borne, work for work, labor for labor, governed by the *simple law of equivalents*. Whatsoever apart from this, a violation of equity and a wrong, resulting in the subjugation and slavery of the party wronged—*a curse alike to both parties*.

"Now, what is capital? I have my own definition. *It is a labor-product unused in the day's living; that which is left over.* You may apply this to land, houses, tools, cattle, whatever creature or thing you have to do with. As an exchangeable commodity or thing, *the measuring price is the sum of the labor it represents*. And when it is used, it has no right to make any demand in excess of itself. That is, John Verity has a surplus labor-product of five years. It is his capital. He starts a business. To conduct this business, he must exchange this surplus labor-product for other labor-products. To make the exchange an equitable one, he must render equivalent for equivalent. In this way capital always retains its labor-function. It can honorably invest itself with no other. In his sense capital (as undersood at present) does not exist. It is abolished as robbery. For what is its present demand? Why, it says: 'I am entitled to more than equivalents in making my exchange with other kinds of labor.' This something more is profit, rent, usury or interest. These things must go."

"What will be left?" Swinton gasps. The thought is new to him. "Without rent, who would build houses? Without profit, who would do business? Without interest, who would lend? Don't you mean rather that these compensations shall not be exorbitant? Not that they shall go, but be made more just?"

"What is more just? While they remain as the adjunct of capital, who can tell what just is? You have no measure."

"I do not understand."

"No; no more than I did at first. It took me some time to realize that building houses for rentals, doing business for profit, loaning money for interest—all might cease, and yet the world get on just as well, business equal to all demands be done—the incentive just as strong and far more honorable."

"Well, explain."

"Well, I start with the idea that the world is always equal to the emergency; knows how, when it reaches a point in its evolution, to make the shift—take its new ideas and put them into practice. This country furnishes a good illustration in its political course. That the source of power lay in the people, and not in the divine right of kings, was an idea that revolutionized institutions, forms, customs, in a manner, at the time, quite as startling as any change now proposed. We have had religious and political revolutions tending to establish democracy in Church and State; now, to complete the trinity, we need this industrial revolution, emancipation. Though it comes to the front last in the order of time, it really is the foundation of both the others. To utter and vote *convictions*, it is, to say the least, far better to have one's bread and butter made sure. But, of course, it all goes on together. It all means progress, growth—the perfection of the race—'democracy triumphant,' to use the phrase of Andrew Carnegie. He—blind man that he is—shouts victory, triumph, when the battle is only just on. He hasn't got down to the real issue involved in the problem of democracy.

" But to come back to the point. You see, I am chuck full, as the boys say, and, in an off hand conversation so, feel I may be allowed a greater latitude—run off for a word or two hither and yon.

" The point is, what shall we do if we give up these privileges claimed as the necessary rewards of capital—without which capital, it is asserted, would soon be a thing of the past, because men would not save that for which they had no speculative use? The answer my common sense at once furnishes me is, men will continue to supply their needs after as before. If they want houses, they will build them. If they want employment—and all men do, or should—they will seek it, each after his own gift. And every man's property shall represent his own labor, or a bequest   It is no worse for capitalists to give over their plunder than for highwaymen on land, or pirates on sea."

" When it is shown that it is plunder? "

" Precisely. You have a logical mind, young man, and drive me on to saying the right thing. I have been dwelling on the results of the present use of capital; attempting to make it clear that this use, as surely as day follows night, or night day, brought about the class distinction of rich and poor; robs the many for the enrichment of the few. No man who does not call to his aid this toll-gathering function permitted to capital can make a fortune, as the phrase is. His wits may go far, but without his profits and his rents and his usury, no exclusive, princely fortune can be realized.

"So much for the claim that the system is wrong, as shown by results. Now for reasons based on the principle of the thing: the *ethical side founded in right reason.*

"Everybody will assent to the statement that in all honorable dealing there should be equivalents rendered; that the scales should balance; that one should 'get his money's worth.' We assent to this, and straightway go and see in what ways we can get the best of the bargain. As it seems to me, it all comes about in this way.

16

"We have come to think it a legitimate thing in business to take advantage of one another's ignorance and misfortune In placing a price on a thing we wish to sell we look at the would be purchaser and say to ourselves : '*What does he know about it ?*' or, '*How much does he desire it?*' In other words, 'How bad off is he? What is his strait?' Then we 'sock it to him.' "

"Oh, no! not so bad as that !" cried Swinton, laughing. "For most things there is now a uniform price."

"You are right and wrong both. In every case where there is a one or uniform price, it is where competition has held the natural greed in restraint. There is no principle in it ; no sense of equity. Simply the practice of a little prudence. If your tradesman wants to keep your trade, he must either give you a superior article, or keep his price as low as his neighbor's. A man in New Bedford, Massachusetts, once found out that the supply of matches was likely to be limited. He made a small fortune by buying out all his competitors and putting up the price to the point where he thought people would not prefer to go with unlighted pipes or sit in the dark. The same thing goes on constantly. It's a case of how bad off your neighbor is, regulated by competitors in the same line of business. The motto on the flag is : '*A thing is worth what it will bring.*' Not a touch of humanity beneath its folds, not an iota of equity. It is the flag of the pirate, and should always be painted black.

"Change this for Josiah Warren's dictum : '*Cost the limit of price.*' What it *costs* the seller to deliver the article, whatever it may be. How much time, how much outlay. The question of another's financial strait does not enter into the calculation, cuts no figure. If he can pay for the article, that's all. The dealer says : ' Here, I'm so much out. Make me whole again.' "

" Ah ! but how does he get on, if he simply keeps on being made whole again ?"

" Why, his own time and labor has been included in the cost, hasn't it ? He gets on that much. What more is he entitled to ?"

" And his capital counts for nothing ?"

"Counts for as much as it ever did. It is kept intact. At the end of five years, say, he has the same capital he began with, with the addition of all his labor-product he has saved over his expenses."

" That is, he uses his capital, and gets no more than any other laborer who has no capital ?"

" Why should he ? He is using his capital to help himself to further work."

" But he helps others, benefits them ; why should he not be rewarded for that ?"

"Why should he claim any reward beyond the burden borne ? Can you tell me ? Mind you, he is not making demands for the *benefit* he is doing *another*, but for the *cost to himself.* The outlay to preserve and operate his capital comes into the cost. But why should he say to the man whom he wishes to work for him : ' See here, I give you employment.

17

You ought to give me a bonus for your chance. I do you a great benefit. Pay for that.' The answer might well be: 'Like an honest man, I will make good all loss your enterprise necessitates for my sake, and we will exchange labor for labor.'

"I do not here go into the question as to whether one man's labor is worth more than another man's, measured by time. That is important, but not necessarily involved in the phase of the subject we are considering. The question is, whether all transactions of business should not rest solely on a labor basis—on the cost in labor of production and delivery—and not involve an imaginary compensation for service in the shape of benefits or favors. Using capital is one thing; the cost of using, another. The *use* does not involve price beyond the *cost*.

"It all turns on that—on the labor-cost."

"I see light breaking through the darkness very gently!" cried Swinton, laughing. "But I must confess you seem to have led me into a labyrinth of speculation, and I don't just know whether we shall go on to open day or retreat to the old world again."

"I think you will find the retreat henceforth closed upon you. The human mind hitched to a star of however gentle light keeps on its course to the dawning day."

"Then, if I understand you, all profit and rent in excess of cost is unjust—is, in point of fact, robbery?"

"Yes, it may be stated so in brief. But that only opens the discussion. Perhaps we have had enough talk for one day. I for one feel my dinner-bell in my stomach. You see, we must all go back to that for a re-lease of life."

Our reporter had gotten all he could carry of the intellectual sort. A good dinner would aid digestion. Yes, he would have a good dinner, and go fishing. Let capital and labor simmer in his brain as they might. Another morning, refreshed in spirit, his ambition restored to full vigor, he would summon them forth again, and by himself go over the ground again. He would see how he could himself handle the matter alone—whether he had been led away into a realm of pure vision where mere sentiment had run riot, or if in very fact the cost-idea had an earthly abiding-place.

"To dinner now! But thanks, old man—a thousand thanks. If I get on with your ideas, I'll return and let you know."

"If you *don't*, return sure," the old man replied gently, grasping Swinton's extended hand.

"All right. I'll do so whether or no. I see I can catch a train for Pittsburgh. My headquarters are there."

Morning came. Swinton saw the first roseate streakings of the east, but sleep still held command o'er his senses, and he submitted without protest. The forenoon wore away without his waking. The maid had tried the door a number of times and grown impatient with this interruption of her morning's task. She was about to report the case to the office, when her trained ear caught the sound of a stir within.

A quiet noon lunch, and our reporter, contrary to his predetermination of the evening before, strolls toward the depot. An hour later he sits in the shade on the river-bank and sees the old man, with a smile on his fine face, quietly approaching. He had not noticed the day before how strong and noble the face was—so serene, hopeful, assured, believing, it seemed. Sleep doubtless had performed its good offices for the old man as well.

The conference lasted until the shadows of evening fell on the scene.

There was more to say.

Another appointment was made, and yet others—on into another week.

But there are limits to everything. Our report of this reporter cannot be the exception. What further may have passed between our friends—for friends they are now—to the writer, at least—who can withhold admiration and love from souls such as theirs, men who pause joyfully by the wayside to brood over the world's hopes and aspirations, animated only by "enthusiasm of humanity," from which flows finally all the progress and glory of our race?

Hold your opinions, convictions, old man, however visionary or o'erturning they do seem. The spirit brooding ever o'er your meditations sanctifies all.

And you, Swinton, young man—you without prejudices, prejudgments, but with open mind to read, and heart to treasure truth only—heaven speed you and deliver you of your message finally for the world's great good ! Who can tell but from such as you shall come the deliverance we seek ?

But the nature of the message written in full, forming the document over which the editor and the wife sat in contemplation serious and earnest enough nigh one whole night—that yet remains in the safe keeping of the editorial sanctum.

The *Western Commonwealth* has gone steadily on its course for two months now, giving no sign the public may heed of a change of heart.

The wife had been heard to say to a neighbor wife: "My husband agrees with your husband so far as this : there is a labor problem. He began the study of it thinking he had an easy task. He thought he could dispose of it in a few bright editorials. How easy to write something owl-wise and smart, as other editors do ! He showed me one such, and I begged him to put it in the fire. It never appeared. I don't know when the labor question will be discussed again in the columns of the *Commonwealth ;* but some time it will be—will be *discussed*, not *disposed* of."

There is nothing left for us but patient waiting. But that waiting is charged with expectation and hope. The *Western Commonwealth!* Never was there a better name. How readily may it be made to stand for the common weal of the great Western world ! And is the time not fitting—as we celebrate now the victory of Columbus?

*   *   *   *   *   *   *   *

Since writing the above, a bit of fortune has fallen to me. Lodged by chance in the same room of the hotel where young

Swinton made his stay in Pittsburgh, I yielded to an old habit of looking into the drawers of the stands and bureaus. I have often so discovered some old shred of a newspaper or leaves of a book with item or two of interest which I could carry away for use some time. On the occasion referred to, the drawer in the stand contained a profusion of "rubbish" which the maid had not set eyes on, evidently. How fortunate!

At first sight I exclaimed to myself: "This, now, may be a very interesting if not sacred deposit of Swintonian literature."

The reader may believe that I lost no time in prosecuting my investigation.

But alas! I found only odds and ends—nothing that could possibly be of the slightest consequence to anybody in earth or heaven.

But, as I gave up my search, and drew forth a half sheet of newspaper that lay in the bottom of the drawer, out of its folds fell two or three scraps of paper which looked suspiciously like being something. I fancied that they had an air of importance as they fluttered to the floor.

Enough. I rescued them, deciphered them, and this is the result.

Important— The reader shall judge.

FIRST MEMORANDA.

1. Homestead strike not in it. Successful or not, no result affecting solution of labor issue.

2 (Aside.) Pinkerton's band should be broken up like other private bands that let themselves to do murderous work. This, or else free competition, and the whole police work of the country turned over to private enterprise—answerable in their work for all manner of misdemeanor.

3. The labor issue turns on the usurpations of capital. The gist of which is—the demand for hours of labor without, so to speak, a labor-return.

4. Capital used at cost. Whatever labor it costs to manipulate it, enters into price, nothing more. No price for benefits or favors.

5. Settles the land question. Price of land—cost of labor improvement. Put posts around a thousand acres and call them yours? Nonsense! You are not even entitled to pay for your labor in planting your posts. No earthly use to any one else; no, nor to yourself. You can ask another to pay for your folly. Land to be sold or exchanged must have a labor-basis No labor, no price. Not *land* sold or exchanged, after all, but *labor*.

So with everything. Not the thing, but the labor in it, should settle price.

6. "My necessities are great. I must have it at any price." Honest answer: "I know nothing of your necessities. I measure my price by my own sacrifice."

This idea of a *cost-price* as against a *value-price* starts a thousand questions, most of them arising, however, from the state of things under the old or *value* system. To say, "I set price according to *cost* to me, not *value* to you," upsets all the calculations of the present piratical business program.

7. No matter—since it furnishes, approximately, at least, an answer to the question, what is a fair day's pay for a fair day's work? The reply being, "Another fair day's work, of course." The Carnegies take heed.

8. Equality, liberty, fraternity, to be realized politically, socially, industrially, if ever Democracy is triumphant.

9. What equality, what liberty, what fraternity are : studies for everybody.

10. Warren's idea—that to harmonize you must first individualize everybody and everything—worthy of profound consideration.

11. Instead of *union*, we must look for *harmony*. The individual notes must preserve their separate individual tones : so together co-operating, sound the grand anthem of Democratic life, liberty, peace.

* * * * * *

Consider the matter at length under the following heads :

1. Exchange of labor, including time and skill.
2. Competition under cost-system.
3. Money.
4. Organization.
5. Co-operation.

Office of *The Western Commonwealth.*
September 1, 1892.

Dear Mr. Swinton :—My husband has been too busy to give you the answer he desires to your communication on the labor issue. The board of directors held your communication in consideration, meeting daily, for over a week. While appreciating the ability with which you have presented the many points involved (and catching, I imagine, in spite of themselves, something of the enthusiasm your advocacy of the new movement must inevitably inspire in all minds), they decide that the *Western Commonwealth* should not enter the list to lead the new reform until the whole matter of the workingman's reward has been more thoroughly canvassed. Mr. Parringham says: "Swinton may congratulate himself, at least, that the journal has by his communication been held in check, and has not gone off on a crusade of 'Nationalism,' as was almost determined on. His report called a halt, and compelled the directors to canvass the whole matter anew." My husband is himself in some uncertainty of mind, for which he owes you many thanks. I write at his request to say that he will always appreciate your great service to himself and the *cause.* You see he has come to say "*cause.*" Three months ago he was sure there was *no* cause, *no* labor issue worthy attention, unless it was to rid the country of tramps by making every such person *show cause* why he was not earning an honest living. He has traveled far enough away from that idiotic frame of mind now.

One of the directors sent him in to-day two or three queries suggested by your communication, which he turns over to you for reply.

Of one thing you may rest assured—revolutions, once started, never turn back. The *Commonwealth* is in the "swim," to use the, I believe, English word, and we may expect great things. The journal has a financial backing that places it above pecuniary difficulties, if the owners once decide on however unpopular a course. To our surprise, they have developed a decided missionary zeal. Once embarked, they will, as one of them has affirmed, spend their last dollar to make their journal a great power for good. And let me assure you that "last dollar" is at the bottom of a very big pile. As earnest of this phase find enclosed a check for five hundred.

Yours very sincerely,
Martha Parringham.

Young Swinton was vastly pleased by the receipt of the above letter. The money enclosure did not come amiss, but the absolutely friendly tone of the note reassured and comforted him. How is it that a man never enters on any great work of elevating import to humanity but noble women come forth to meet him with greetings and encouragement? In his lonely brain man follows along the line of some high impulse, announces a new conviction. Forthwith steps a woman to say: "I believe it; I know it; I have known it all along in my heart." And then, her only ambition to carry the idea to the ends of the earth! The reply of that judge who, when asked his opinion of the young Emerson, could only confess: "Oh, I don't pretend to understand him, but my daughters do," but states a fact paralleled times untold. The daughters, the women, are early and late with the world's best thought and purpose. No sepulchre can entomb their faith. The cause is never lost. It cannot be. The universe is not so fashioned.

It is not improper here to declare that Martha Parringham may be ranked with the world's most intelligent and lovable natures.

The interrogatories to which Swinton must find answers were:

1. If socialism or communism are not advisable, how is co-operation possible? Co-operation by profit-sharing is ruled out by the interdiction of profit. How does individualism co-operate?

2. If capital is not to be owned and managed by a few capable men, will there be any capital to manage? Distributed among the million, how will it be brought into service for individual enterprises where there must be stability and freedom of action on the part of managers?

3. In the practical working of the doctrine of labor for labor, will the inequality in abilities be disregarded? In other words, is capability to be set aside, and every man's time to be declared of equal value with every other man's?

4. What about money?

5. Is competition done away with?

6. If not, does not your *cost*-idea land you back just where you started, with *value* the ruling consideration?

Eager enough for the argument, Swinton soon realized how much easier it must be to ask than to answer questions. He had written a whole chapter on each number. The floor was covered with manuscript. But that would never do. He must boil it down. Compact in the smallest compass possible, the directors could spin the thing out for themselves. He could only give texts. They must go on with the sermons. In fact, he argued, if they could not of themselves work out the problem from a few hints, why, they were off the track entirely, and he could not switch them on. But once on the track, keen for the scent as he was, they could, as he had done, follow the business on to the end.

His letter finally ran as follows:

DEAR MRS. PARRINGHAM:—How can I tell you of the pleasure the receipt of your note, with its enclosure of "funds" and the "queries" of directors, has afforded me? The "funds" came not amiss, and the answers I am expected to give to points of so much interest add new stimulus to my pen, an instrument which ought to be in these days in everybody's hand "mightier than the sword." But it is your confidence in me and your support of this new phase of the labor question that yields me the greatest satisfaction. I turn to my task with added zest and delight.

I will reply to the directors, rearranging questions as follows :

1. *Exchange of labor involving time and skill.*

Labor for labor measured by time—contrary as it is to prevailing custom, where *value* instead of *cost* establishes price—does not seem other than as it should be in a community of friends where *equity* is the ideal.

Why *should* one man's time measure more than another's? All have the same natural demands to supply by their labor. It does not follow from this that one with a profession or trade which has cost a previous outlay of time and means must give time, in a present exchange, hour for hour, with another man's time whose labor has not called for the same preparation. If five years have been given necessarily to learning a trade, these five years enter into the cost of the labor-exchange. The other man must foot up a like cost to render his equivalent. If he has only to take a spade and dig the ground at will with no previous cost in training, he will give more present labor in exchange than the man who has to make good his past outlay. This matter may not be adjusted to a feather's weight ; it is enough that the intention is there, and that equity is sought for.

As to unequal abilities, that consideration must settle itself, as it now does. The competent in competition with the incompetent : those who can do a given task with least outlay in time, set the cost-price.

2. This brings me to the query, "Is competition done away with?" That would be as impossible as undesirable. While differences in ability exist—and such differences are probably to abide with the human race forever—the competitive system as to skill and adaptabilty must go on, not only as incentive, but as benefit to all by reduction of cost. Result, less labor, and better work. Competitive ability is one prime factor of civilization.

But competitive starvation, which now enters so largely into establishment of price, under the reign of *cost*-idea will disappear. When a business is overcrowded by workers, there are remedies. Say, first, if the supply of an article manufactured is already equal to demand, workers must turn to other employments. A labor bureau of statistics should be able to furnish all needed data to regulate demand and supply in all departments of industry for the world. If there be more laborers than labor required for established enterprises, what is more apparent than that new industries must be opened up ? The tendency would constantly be toward each worker's finding and fitting himself to his task.

And then, under a reign of equity, fewer hours a day would serve for supplying the laborer's demands. No longer robbed of a "fair day's pay for a fair day's work," the labor-day could be lessened in time, and other demands of the civilizing man be met. Demand for more laborers would thereby increase, to supply demand for production.

3. *Money.* The simple, controlling idea in producing money, it seems to me, should be to keep it, as now, a medium of exchange ; only, there should be a *labor*-dollar, furnished at *cost*—calling for a specified service, and backed by satisfactory securities. Not by any means a *fiat*-money, but something akin in idea to the gold-basis of present money. Not government fiat or government monopoly, but free competition. It is an I O U always of so much labor, payable on demand. The labor may have been already performed, or it may be a promise of future labor. A mere matter of convenience that must be kept down to cost of production. Bankers not as speculators, but as laboring men, and like all other men entitled to their hire, or *equivalents.*

Only a general idea—but a working idea, it seems to me.

4. *Co-operation.* If one works at his own task, accomplishes it faithfully and well, it follows of necessity that he is co-operating with all others who do the same thing to add to the common or mutual welfare. In conducting large enterprises requiring hundreds of men—no one man having capital sufficient—he, the competent leader or proprietor, must needs borrow of his fellow-laborers. He is thus selected or elected as the man among others best equipped to conduct the affair successfully. He must be absolute owner of the concern, and be able individually to manage without interference. The support given implies this confidence. The concern is thus individualized ; competency and responsibility placed. The business conducted on the cost-idea, the distribution not of *profit*, but of *product*, goes steadily on in ratio to labor performed by all employed, including employer and employees. Time for time, burden for burden ; the employer employing *himself*, as well as other laborers.

That such a concern would work without friction of any sort is not contended. But that the amount of confusion, contention, strife, engendered by equal co-partnership—a whole army of men and women privileged to assert at every emergency by voice and vote his or her necessarily incompetent opinion—would be far greater and wholly disastrous, the history of all such communistic enterprises abundantly shows. The principle of commanding officers with separate tasks, and workers in subordination, illustrated in military affairs, holds good in all human affairs. Each to his individual task, and this within its limits sovereign. Where no compulsion is used, no one can blame other than himself if he finds himself in a disagreeable position. The way for liberation is always open.

Thus much in brief.

Of course, a thousand and one objections may be raised, not so much against the principle set forth, as to its supposed impracticability. " It won't work " sums up the general verdict of opposition.

But it is the old story.

Nothing *ever works*—in the minds of the vast majority wedded to an old system—whatever it may be.

25

But, in spite of all this doubt and protest, how many things *have* worked completely!

We are born doubters of newness and change. A wise conservatism it may be that in most cases gives things grown up or established a fair show, and keeps the world from flying into pieces.

But now and then a few persons make escape into belief in ideas and principles; stand by them, proclaim them, experiment with them; overcome old obstructions and new ones; live down prejudices and all manner of revilement or persecution; or, dying, leave the world to end its opposition by acceptance.

Of course, because so many good results have been brought about in this fashion, it does not follow that each new idea that comes floating into notice is bound to share the same or similar fortune.

The cost-idea must, like all others, run its course and be glorified or otherwise. Since Warren first launched the proposition, over half a century has elapsed. It is in its favor that events and the world's thinking have steadily, if slowly, been driven on to conclusions familiar to him in those early years. Like the other Warren at Bunker Hill, he fell while the battle was yet on, gloriously struggling. America may yet concede noble results flowing from his devotion and sacrifice.

I am conscious of having touched merely the great problem, and with no skillful hand. But it does seem to me, Mrs. Parringham, that all our traditions, as well as our ideals, which distinguish our new world from the elder worlds, are leading on to the freedom and equity the old man at Homestead, following in Warren's footsteps, ceaselessly, assuredly proclaims.

I am very sincerely yours,

RALPH SWINTON.

This supplementary chapter brings the "Narrative by the Wayside" up to date.

CPSIA information can be obtained
at www.ICGtesting.com
Printed in the USA
LVHW082057300321
683007LV00002B/39